This superb collection offers up history—personal, familial, postcolonial, geopolitical, ecological—and indeed the history of fruit, fruit as sustenance, pleasure, exploitable product, as image, parent, love, and wound, "this singular / ripening sweetness, the pleasure and // the horror of it / like a tree so globe-laden // its branches snap / under the weight of it." There is no eating fruit without decimating its wholeness, and it is this split, especially in regard to the speaker's bifurcated racial and cultural identity, that generates the book's intricate architecture and vitality: "I live in a time of competing utopias / There is one wherein the seas stay put   and one / wherein everyone looks like me." "What does it mean, anyway, to live in a country? I wouldn't know…" The sweep of the language is Pangeaic. It is lush and theoretical, intimate and epic, at times elevated, and then tender, and then conversational. "Is it all right if I just go ahead and say / that the moral of this story / will have something to do / with the scourge of capitalism? Will you keep reading? / Good okay   then—" The formal variety is remarkable without calling too much attention to itself. There is a sestina, a ghazal, an erasure, and rhyming couplets, poems riven and seamed, and lines with white space gaps as visual caesura, even a form that emulates "a videocamera that fell out of a plane and landed in a pig trough," but the experiments arise organically from each poem's purpose and particular emotional hue.

Despite the love that the speaker expresses, her realm is existential loneliness, and she owns it. "It turns out that any constellation   can lead you astray," she writes, "that any sky   can ask you I'm sorry   do I know you." Still, her poems do not spin in a cosmic fog. They are solidly placed. In Manila, where the rains are so persistent that "roofs become radios, the gray noise sweeping every   room with a broom made of profound differences." On American rivers, "their greenish syntax letting all the silk / slip to the floor." In her grandmother's kitchen, "the aproned comma of my lola cleaning squid…the smell of the sea—the presence of death, / the preservative of salt—laying its net upon my face." In an American hunting camp, "(w)hich is a man's / place, a white man's place. Which inheritance, / which 'tradition,' which deed marked 1804 stashed / in the floorboards. Which America." These are hard-won poems, fought for, lived through. They do not resolve; to resolve would equal self-abandonment. Nor do they locate or repair the single center that will not hold. Instead they inventory a parallel history—"Raspberry, cherry, coconut, santol, passionfruit (dislike), apricot, lychee, mango, blueberry. So many different centers." The history of fruit.

—Diane Seuss, 2018 Akron Poetry Prize judge

AKRON SERIES IN POETRY
Mary Biddinger, Editor

Kimberly Quiogue Andrews, *A Brief History of Fruit*
Joshua Harmon, *The Soft Path*
Oliver de la Paz, *The Boy in the Labyrinth*
Krystal Languell, *Quite Apart*
Brittany Cavallaro, *Unhistorical*
Tyler Mills, *Hawk Parable*
Caryl Pagel, *Twice Told*
Emily Rosko, *Weather Inventions*
Emilia Phillips, *Empty Clip*
Anne Barngrover, *Brazen Creature*
Matthew Guenette, *Vasectomania*
Sandra Simonds, *Further Problems with Pleasure*
Leslie Harrison, *The Book of Endings*
Emilia Phillips, *Groundspeed*
Philip Metres, *Pictures at an Exhibition: A Petersburg Album*
Jennifer Moore, *The Veronica Maneuver*
Brittany Cavallaro, *Girl-King*
Oliver de la Paz, *Post Subject: A Fable*
John Repp, *Fat Jersey Blues*
Emilia Phillips, *Signaletics*
Seth Abramson, *Thievery*
Steve Kistulentz, *Little Black Daydream*
Jason Bredle, *Carnival*
Emily Rosko, *Prop Rockery*
Alison Pelegrin, *Hurricane Party*
Matthew Guenette, *American Busboy*
Joshua Harmon, *Le Spleen de Poughkeepsie*

Titles published since 2011.
For a complete listing of titles published in the series,
go to www.uakron.edu/uapress/poetry.

A Brief History of Fruit

Kimberly Quiogue Andrews

The University of Akron Press
Akron, Ohio

ISBN: 978-1-629221-61-8 (paper)
ISBN: 978-1-629221-62-5 (ePDF)
ISBN: 978-1-629221-63-2 (ePub)

LIBRARY OF CONGRESS CATALOGING-IN-PUBLICATION DATA

Names: Andrews, Kimberly Quiogue, 1983- author
Title: A brief history of fruit / Kimberly Quiogue Andrews.
Description: First edition. | Akron, Ohio : The University of Akron Press, 2020. | Series: Akron series in poetry
Identifiers: LCCN 2019046213 | ISBN 9781629221618 (paperback ; alk. paper) | ISBN 9781629221625 (ePDF) | ISBN 9781629221632 (ePub)
Subjects: LCGFT: Poetry.
Classification: LCC PS3601.N552665 B75 2020 | DDC 811/.6—dc23
LC record available at https://lccn.loc.gov/2019046213

Cover image: *Fruits (Watermelon & Passionfruit)* by Debbie Carlos. Used with permission. Cover design by Amy Freels.

A Brief History of Fruit was designed and typeset in Garamond, with Univers display, by Amy Freels and printed on sixty-pound natural and bound by Bookmasters of Ashland, Ohio.

Produced in conjunction with the University of Akron Affordable Learning Initiative. More information is available at www.uakron.edu/affordablelearning/

Contents

III.

IV.

V.

nts, and theirs.

Friction

: the agitation, the Spanish, hardwood door
that wears and wears its paler path against
dark varnish on the floor.

I.

*We might want to believe that we can condemn and we can love
and we can condemn because we love our country,
but that's too complex.*

Still Life with Metalworking Shop

(Central Pennsylvania, ca. 1960)
(Ink on paper)

In this scene, we can see that the catalogue of the gone records itself among the catalogue of what remains. The objects resting in partial shadow upon the higher shelves (a single heatproof glove, fourteen nails in a box marked "Pepsi-Cola," fluid in a jar) most readily draw the eye, creating a sense of mystery but also directing the gaze eventually downward, as if through layers of soil. Particularly evocative in this instance—not often found in the still life, artists preferring the fruits of the hunt, or as is well known, literal fruit—are the boxes and boxes of relatively small-caliber bullets slotted into a custom-built storage unit, indicating that this shop was used almost exclusively for the fashioning of rifles. Suggestive of the card catalogues that once lined library walls, the array of ammunition invites the viewer to think about the organizational qualities of violence. An oiled rag indicates attention to detail. Questions for art educators: how does this scene juxtapose nostalgia and the domination of man over nature? What physical sensations are evoked by the hard lines of the anvil in the lower right-hand side of the frame? How do those sensations contrast with those produced by the empty, wheeled wooden chair, center off-left, rolled slightly away from a desk upon which rest yet more bullets, some graph paper, writing utensils, and other things now lost to the mind trying to retrieve this picture for the viewer? How do you think the owner of this chair might react if his son married someone who was not white? If you or a family member has ever aimed a gun at an animal, perhaps the array of tools scattered about the scene will hold a special meaning. You can write these down on paper, and they will become a bouquet of pheasants, flushed and fleeing.

Ars Persona

A frozen orange, a goldfinch, a peach.
No one ever uses a ray gun to make things bigger,
so here I am, digesting thistle seed, each a tome,
a vessel overfloweth, a familial tumult of windows.
The peace we make with the panes of the past,
their glass. I was born with a purpose, to rustle vaguely,
shed like a palm, languidly. There goes
one spent brown thing, there goes a network
of fibers of no more use to my musculature. Growing
into the neutral singular involves lying
about consistency, as in, "my feet were always feet"
and never the yellow slick of mango on a held spoon,
never a palm full of lead pellets plucked from a squirrel.
The appliqué *I* has good posture at parties.
See it leaning into you, asking about
your coin collection? I am holding against my chest
a disassembly of split wood and straw,
scales and the procession of seasonal fruition.
In the company of so much invention, it would be
easy to say that I never show up alone, that it's always
me *and* my potluck dish *and* this friend of mine
from another planet. Searching for something
to stand in for estrangement from my own skin,
I read transliterations of birdcalls:
What need, what need, what need?
Bay-bee—yes, that when all this flesh gathers
on the widening sill, the globe of it will orbit
with stupendous precision, will hold forth in loud
perpetuity. Sometimes I hear it as a name
shouted in recognition. Other times,
as the liquid roar of a heaven in which
everyone can have the juice of an orange
without splitting it first.

n: Shield, or Shell Covering

The differing suns. Exploratory comparator of memory's carapace.
Prone under the dome of a North American sky: its sheen, my carapace.

The snow reshuffles itself on the windowsill. A love poem
for drawn-out Decembers, their blue-white and crystalline carapace.

Take the banana leaf. As package, as platter, as durable as the Filipino heat
from which it unfurls, broadly, a readymade. Sweet rice, green carapace.

Swaddling provides a newborn with a sense of the womb's safety.
I fold countries around myself, false familiarity, some serene carapace.

Not, not, not —a litany, a robin, red-breasted indictment of every handful
of soil I try to hold. It's what the cicada leaves, split clean—a carapace.

Claim *(v):* to unfree; *(n):* that which makes whole, by hook or by crook. Use
in a sentence: I claim my grandmother's island house, a screened carapace.

Even the Philippines has seasons. Its pronouncements are softer, a little
shift from *close* to *closer*. Its leaves shine damply, a stilled beetle's carapace.

Wholly mediated, I step as through a door from room to room, first
a fish, then a hare. Thus my hollows, surrendered, unseen carapace.

Some Unsettling Connections

In Pasig, they put up a barricade of façades
to make every day a kind of Easter—
gaudy resurrections behind which the city
crowds, tin roofs like a completed puzzle
someone has pushed up against a wall. This is all
in order to say, of course, that artifice
is either end of a magnet, depending on who
feels worse that day, you or your imagination.
For me, the latter, no contest—I appreciate
breakfasts of *pandesal* with strawberry jam
and realize that the permanence of dead fish
is not a zero-sum equation. I'm fine; thank you
for asking. But the slant corrugate, the pink
blockade damming it from the street's eyes—
maybe I'll arch over it, gather several banana leaves
on each arm like glossy flight feathers
and wave myself over everything covered
in dust and scales, flail over the thick of it
because nothing that's awkward is worth doing
halfway. I did not intend originally for this
to become a metaphor for loving you, but nor
do I control the color of the fruits you imagine.
Are you afraid of that sweetness? It's all right—
the Pasig River asphyxiates itself nearly daily.
I am made of green things rising despite
themselves, of an uncomfortable wet heat,
and in these sidelong spaces I'm willing
to admit that I would land with a grateful thud
in the bed in the morning, push up against
your turned back, tuck my wings into the space
between our bodies, quiet and differing.

In which I climb a tree, as a child, and find my father's initials about 16 feet off the ground

The seasons' folding in Appalachia bearing witness
to a thousand slow implosions—
broad leaves falling like kneeling benches. An evenly knitted
blanket of maple and clay. In the canopy,
I am a small monkey, fiddling with the end of a stem
in wonder. Yes and no. The cooler reality
wears Keds and rustles slowly skywards. What we feel
when we discover something—expected or unexpected,
the temple you knew was somewhere within your reach or the pleasure
of a bittersweet drink—drives the colonial impulse. Our joy
is rigged.   C   F   A
Individual fault is a terrible entrée into any discussion about nostalgia.
Nevertheless, in the autumn, I search those worn-down mountains
for anything that has not changed,
for an ascension that I can halt, forgive me, by pressing hard with my hands.

How to Get Into a Poem

(Standing Stone Creek, Pennsylvania)

[A startling observation about the nature of human life]
or [A concrete description of trout]
[Backstory, alluding to an individuating experience]
or [Personal background, like "I have a weird relationship
to rural America"]
[Imagery only loosely related to backstory/background]
[Plants]
[Fruits]
or [Tropical fruits if part of you is tropical]
[Some intellectual discourse on the word "part"]
or [Agonized associative thinking about the nature
of something politically urgent, like colorism]
[A return to the opening vignette so folks stay on track,
like "is it possible that a suburban mixed kid actually
has nothing at all to claim, not the trout, not the breadfruit"]
[A direction, e.g. "towards"]
or [A time, e.g. "now" or "after"]
[A prepositional or noun phrase if grammatically necessary]
[A turn, which should also be startling, as in *oh
this is what the poem is really about*]
or [Imagery that achieves roughly this purpose, like that of
the properties of brackish water,
or the length and nature of brackish days]

On Labor

(Belgrade Lakes, Maine)

The long days of summer are a false solace. More time
awake means more time to witness your dreams' fodder.

At the small lakeside cabin that my grandfather built
("like a brick shithouse"—my own father, grumbling,

struggling to budge thick cedar planking off of a chest
full of sheets), I once watched a boyfriend take it upon

himself to clean out the old aluminum canoe, perched
on its tiny horses next to the shed.
                                        One way to explain

the enormous appeal of Gustav Klimt's paintings might be
to argue that his faces are essentially melancholic

surrounded by the ecstatic: the real, that is, emerging
in a certain flesh-tone out of a sea of gold and green.

I am not a woman in a patterned yellow dress. My face
is, however, covered by this hand. Polycrystalline and growing,

the moment forms itself from salt and sugar, all those
parallel edges. In *The Three Ages of Woman*, it is the hag

who appears pregnant.
                        The decades of my brain produce
the men in this story: the *pater familias*, either one, in a cove

into which I cannot reach; the boyfriend, carrying the canoe atop
his bare shoulders, staggering slightly under its weight,

a tottering tipped vessel grown legs and out, out—
onto the lake. Men, a mosaic. The desperately

uncomfortable eroticism of this memory of work—
his steadying arms, the kneeling, the motions of small waves

against aluminum and a heavy sponge against neglect's
many accumulations. The shifting of musculature under

skin, the promise, as I took it, of an ability to force
the rocks along the shore back together in the thin spring,

after the ice steals in, expands in its usual way,
cracks even the hardest surfaces, then turns again to water.

Ode to the Letter Q

(not after Sharon Olds)

A quail, bobbing in its variegated affirmative
        (or trembling, a contraction of air and space
        like something plummeting)—

what strangeness allows, what "I see," what "what"
        in the plumage of a kickstand—
        unfathomable as closets, perched, propped

on top of a slanted shelf, O with ornament
        I wear upon my head to signal the deep brown
        of my eyes and hair as rooted, as reckoning,

hello, squinting, *hello*, "what kind of name is that"
        though not unkindly, a registration, a record—
        round magnification of my value, lovely

derivative, the shape of a palette of paint
        (surface blended to a uniform beige)—
        a hollow with a handle, a scoop with which

to fish my mother out from the deep pool of my
        embodied whiteness, this is not a poem
        about printing the dead but rather an attempt

to show you the two small beasts that I keep in my hands.

Love's Varietal

: a smooth Noblesse, the way
you keep saying that every time you write

about fruit
you mean *father*

bowl of father: skin of father
the nectarine's pale flesh, changeling peel

the matte of it
a bunch of father: father tree

his love of stone fruits, their gathering
sugars, such that

you wish every month were June, in all
the sun's enormity, no

matter that
a nectarine is pink ovary swollen

no matter this
hollow pit this pocket of seed only this:

this singular
ripening sweetness, the pleasure and

the horror of it
like a tree so globe-laden

its branches snap
under the weight of it

In a different sky, on a different night

For as long as the stars do not seem to align in an orderly manner, as long as
such lost light sources make their way into the spinning crevices of her lungs,
she will continue to ask herself: How does one make a habitation of it?
—*Jennifer S. Cheng*

A flock of geese   blots out the stars
flicking them in and out of the sky   in brief
wingbeaten increments   Orion's triplicate sash
then just a buckle   then again its small hill

The capriciousness of the visible   my back to beaches
I divide my time   neatly into temperate fourths
When my life   is hopeless
I invent a field   called comparative astronomy

For instance   Hawaii is the only state in the union
whose skies display   at certain times   The Crux
or southern cross   The main disciplinary assumption
in other words   is that each place

has its own sky   at each place
will interpret   an inverted instrument   of torture
in flame   above its head   in a different way
We don't see it up here   in the white north

we see an upright bear   the arrow of conquest
no scorpions curling their tails   down towards us
Meantime   the only Catholic country
in Southeast Asia   lies flung across the water

under the heat   that sections me off
pushed through the sieve   of my undoing recollection
It turns out that any constellation   can lead you astray
that any sky   can ask you I'm sorry   do I know you

Apostrophe

Mother, apart from everything, I have gone looking for you, as you must have known and as you must continue to know. The color of searching and also of the darkness is blue, the blue leaves and their bluer underbellies. The blue boat of the coming dawn. Night remains itself, cooler in some places than in others; its generative nature remains also, despite the already-gone quality of starlight.

I have wanted to explain certain things about the difference between the brain and the body. Not that I'm some sort of Cartesian dualist, but we also choose neither the shell nor the way in which it is received in the world. Sometimes we think we can hide the body in work. Sometimes the body becomes honored in work, as in "Filipinos are really hard workers." Oftentimes that honor lies in wait like a cartoon trap covered in leaves. The leaves are blue, or they are ordinary green and brown.

And then the mind works too hard when the body does not have to. When the body, for instance, has been constructed as neutral. When I desired to become more specifically utterable and less like the sound of tides, a mild *whoosh*, you were alarmed. You disguise your alarm as nonchalance which exacerbates my generalized anxiety. You say "you're like barely Filipino; I don't even feel Filipino," and I want to say "Filipina, mom" but instead both my spellcheck and the strap around my chest draw a bright red line under my torso.

In the end you have nothing for which to answer, as I have been bad at asking. I remain terrified of the ocean and laugh it off by making jokes about the food chain. Something could just straight up eat you, I say, bobbing along. You could just be subsumed, and no one would know you were ever there.

II.

You don't always know, for instance, that you are lonely.
You may feel free, or stoical, or intrepid.

Did you hear about that video camera that fell out of a plane and landed in a pig trough

There's a big jolt   and then

Field
Sky
Field
Sky

Fieldsky
Fieldsky

Fieldskyfieldskyfieldskyfieldsky

then   remarkably   steady:

Field // Sky

as the camera's spin rate lines up
with its frame rate
and the picture clears

And that's when it hits the ground
and is immediately bitten
by a curious, muttering pig

Now when the edges of my vision
blur a little

East
West

Eastwest etc

I worry   that I too
am milliseconds away
from becoming soup

a map, two points, the line between them

a cough.
in the center of the traffic circle
        on the generally southeast side
           of quezon city

the boy scout memorial
        caged in scaffolding
           salutes vaguely over

some jeepneys

    a swarm of jeepneys

                              a chrome of
                              jeepneys
                                 ?

                   : : :

i'm trying to explain

trying

                                  to
                              explain

                      an angle   a navigation
                  a process : nights like arches
arches : burden capacity (tensile strength)
    "to hold in tension"

                    thesis statement: *come back*

          !!!

a cat eats rice out of a puddle.

                                                        i pocket
                                                        my camera.
                        where are you taking me?   it says.

(the cat.)

this is a problem with the antecedent.

                                ???

starch as scenery (a roundtable) :
long grains   potatoes   what fills us up
papers are welcome on the relationship

                                        between staple food satiation
                                        and the gelling function
                                        of soluble fiber, like
the soft pile of oatmeal
you had
for breakfast, if you did.

if you're into that kind of thing

                                                (eating breakfast)
eating oatmeal for breakfast.

                                ***

saluting as gesture (a lecture) :
to drop

                                                or to grab

                                the hand as nation-builder

                        as seer and acknowledger of shiny things. i
                        marshal my body across an expanse seen by

a metal eye.

: : :

o palm. both the tree
and a hand on a table, upturned,

saying *here*
or *please.*

The Bath

("The Promised Land," a populated waste disposal site
north of Quezon City)

There will be a revolution or there will not. If the latter these poems
were nothing but entertainments.
—Joshua Clover

Efficiency (n): forced scavenging; a boot
on a human face forever and ever amen

I am thumbing the handkerchief in my pocket
I am walking miserably by doorways close and irregular as teeth

And here is the literal trash-fire
And here is the air thick with the smoke of money burned downtown

The name of this place would seem to suggest
that Fukuyama wasn't entirely off-base

But fuck Fukuyama
Refuse refuse being the only imaginable structure

Remember I am walking by doorways
Remember I will now see a child of no more than four

He stands in the doorway damp and covered in soap suds
He has one eye shut against the sting

O world where the scales are so tipped they become a catapult
O the clink of a pail and the metallic clap of water

The maternal presence only arms
The boy squints now with both eyes as the bath comes over him

And the lesson is this
The rinse will be swift and terrible

It will be hair-flattening and dazzling
The dust struck from the air

The Arborist

A peculiar emptiness—
driving down Centre Hall's main street
I suddenly notice that they've cut down all the trees—

"Suburban deforestation"
for when there is no -urban,
just sub-, a neat grid three streets wide along which

shade trees add both color
and value to the nearby properties,
ringed in corn and fallow fields waiting for the next

county fair. And outside
my office, on campus, a giant elm has
simply up and disappeared, a sacrifice to protect

the landscape from
disease. The narcissist asks
Are trees falling in my wake? and the poet does too,

but never the arborist,
who knows that it is a job like
any other: cutting a broad path through the world

and then spending time
in the garden, with tools, methodically
propping up what's left. But there is also the matter

of managing optics.
All this work done in winter
to avoid tree-cutting in the height of summer—

the shaking leaves,
the thin sap flowing freely in the heat.
No one wants to be reminded of the actual nature

of things. Least of all
the poets. In my office I play
at death, give in to those perennial desires: to say

this is *that*.
To read, in the wheat-pale map
the saw leaves behind, my own cartographical wound.

Other Deluges

There are, of course, times in the tropics when you'd think
      it couldn't come down any harder and there's threat
      in that: drowning, or cracking, or the sick wash and
      thud of one followed by the other. There exists also
      a solution into which this precipitates, though I am
      not a chemist, which is obvious. I have lost my book
      of folktales containing the myth of the lanzones fruit,
      the woman pinching away its poison for her child.
      The ants in the kitchen have forced me to store all
      of my cereal in the refrigerator. The rain continues.

And roofs become radios, the gray noise sweeping every
      room with a broom made of hair and difference.
      The startle, then the soothe. All cleaning is simply
      moving something from one place to another. The
      friend with whom I share my bedroom has done
      much more work with postcolonial theory than I
      have and she says "I think it's important that the Fil-
      Am community recognizes the insidious effects of
      decades of hard assimilationism" and I think yes
      it's a real bear explaining to my mother why I am
      here. My mother says why would you want to do that.

Pushing everything downstream, the days pat the place down
      for contraband, leaving Manila's streets warmly slick
      with the grit of passing through in every direction.
      In stories, people move forward, pushing into their own
      spaces as happenings or points. Hands are the hardest
      part of the anatomy to draw because they could look
      like so many other things, none of them human. Hands
      are the reason why I do not draw and this typhoon is
      the reason I am inside placing my forehead gently upon
      a tall stack of paper. Apps for the sleepless use a similar

kind of singly-noted static. Or sometimes a train, which I find baffling because who could possibly fall asleep knowing that a train was coming. I thought the point was to choose from amongst sounds that above all else would not be transient. I thought that all I had to give was a distant ache, like that in the joints before the rain.

How to Read Whitewater in the Mid-Atlantic Region

Here's the gift, the undetermined, toothy space in which it bubbles
up crazily, thrashing around and telling you incessantly about

the nature of possibility: these terrible courtships, in other words,
you've had with rivers, their greenish syntax letting all the silk

slip to the floor. Susquehanna, Lehigh, Youghiogheny, their stolen
clauses, the low trees trailing their fingers as if to say *there now*

river, there now. And in the little canoe, you sound out each line
in turn. This is the side of you that is full of eagles. The story

unfolds in several keenly observed parts: eddies in their indecision.
Standing waves like stacks of letters, each signed *fondly*.

Undercut rocks against which the water boils low and smooth,
dangerous in the same way that simplicity is dangerous—

You read for answers because the painted ceiling above you
demands a key to its own reflection. You read for the sluice

because you are normal: you ask for directions, you are
standard in that finally, you favor the tongue harbored between

the wide-set molars, the sunlight bouncing off of a body
shaped like allowance, like the valleys you dare to call your home.

Acquired Taste

If you've got them, you're supposed to like the "ethnic foods"

of your upbringing. What we want, probably, is an ottoman
with good cushioning, one that keeps us close to but not

exactly on the floor. Earthly feelings are good feelings.

And yet: as a child, I hated my mother's *sinigang*, blinkingly
tart with Knorr's tamarind broth concentrate and full

of radish, pork, beans the length of shoelaces. It tasted like
a knife slicing through a piece of paper. It tasted like the green

part of a sunset, the one everyone squints for and no one
ever actually sees. I have grown into the ability to recognize

the concept of nothing; screens are bad for children because
they render the world untouchable. This is the part where I say

of course I like it now, that my life is sour and analogous foods
make me feel like weights clicking into the right place on a scale.

What I mean is that grief is nothing if not the inability to tell
and retell the beloved of their own significance.

The More Interesting Story

might ostensibly be my white father
in the Philippines   a type of ghost
in that ghosts are scary   and often white
and often representative of past wrongs

it's not any fun   to think of my father this way
he is kind   he is so good to my mother
he brought a sun hat   and swim shorts
and he is frightened really   as opposed
to frightening   the light off the water

the sun with its vengeance   tiny *calamansi*
in all the drinks   this story seems good
I could use   the ocean's depth
to say something about clarity and fear et cetera

there is deep irony   in the phrase
"to be thrown into relief"
my flip-flops   are full   of a sweaty dust
I too   attract crowds   at the fish market

who has written the best analysis   of sympathy
as it relates to kinship   that is   my family
as a lattice crawling with bougainvillea

meanwhile the fig tree balanced   on its tiny trunk
in a pot in every Brooklyn apartment   these days
grows huge in the wild   and bears clusters of fruit

that could be a shock   in its way
as in oh geez   the thing I had contained
has a great green life   of its own
now I'm the small thing   needing watering
now I'm the rock   becoming sand at the shore

The Hunting Camp

(Central Pennsylvania)

Which hangs greater on the eaves. Which sleeps,
striped, which wakes in winter. The Concord vines

on their slanting fence have walked for miles.
Which light, early or late, which interior,

which dust, which selective tilt of the motes' angles,
which forgotten. Which blackened iron pans. Which

antlers, which absent bones, which thin moon.
Which flesh consumed, which hung as trophy, which

burns in autumn or appears to, gathering the torched
tones thrown off the unlayering trees. Which is a man's

place, a white man's place. Which inheritance,
which "tradition," which deed marked *1804* stashed

in the floorboards. Which America. In which
I learn to drive on the brushy expanse of the yard.

Which series of grinding halts. Which scarred
tenderness, which isolated series of tendernesses.

Which weaponry, which disastrous pride, which
brownish progeny in amongst the wood piles—

in which I that progeny steer across the face of it,
knowing what it is, and shift cleanly into second.

III.

Is it possible for this not to be a story of disappearance?

As in Nowhere, No-One

Blue eyes of horses: only occasional, and sightless-
looking, the pale revealing the pupil, fixated
peripherally. Focus, one might say, requires a center,
a straight-ahead. One might think of the prow of a ship.
Below deck, the ocean's entirety presses inward,
the hull remains a sturdy arch, spans
against an infinite weight. You look out the porthole – if
the view is not blue, or green, it is black. You might go back,
then, to thinking about the barn.
                                        Maples turn red without us,
drop leaves that are gathered by nesting squirrels.
"Invisible invisible invisible"
Brown eye: continental slope; the coming of depth. The neither
here nor there, the muzzle so unlike the aqueous slicing
of movement through water, of water through the living.
The whuffling, dawn hours and the smell of straw
become ancient history. Your life: a liner. This is not
the thought that counts. Half-water, half-nail, all salt
on the tongue and in the Pacific, as nutrient and body
seen only in distorted reflections.
                                        How to ride the animal
through both hay and seagrass, into the shape
of a hyphen: don't think too hard about the culinary.
In falling, everything tastes like tannic wind. Leap
over the railing, shove the vertigo into reverse. Swim
towards the bottom. Away from the air.

The Minnow

As we eat we're eaten.
—Li-Young Lee

Permanence in its incarnation, presiding
over the sink: the aproned comma of my lola
cleaning squid. Deftly, her hands moved
between the knife and tentacle, cradled
the clouded mantles. Once,
                              she called
her granddaughter to her work and I came,
the smell of the sea—the presence of death,
the preservative of salt—laying its net upon my face.
Perhaps I was nine. She proffered
                              her palm, small
and smooth as an absence, and into it
I peered to see a squid not-yet-eviscerated,
split from head-fin to siphon and laid open
like a question,
                              tentacles trailing from its body,
gravity-flattened. Inside, a minnow lay, whole
almost to perfection, silver as the sea
in sunlight and staring startled upward.
What did she say,
                              then, to her daughter's daughter,
American child, my grandmother who has seen
so much of the insides of so many things?
I've forgotten. Perhaps it was nothing, silence
bearing the weight
                              refuse. At any rate, I stood in some way,
perhaps agog, fish-like. And in that moment
I would not touch it, that nested predation,
the imagined feel
                              and leavings of it—
mucus or a membrane, the gray odor ghosting
beneath fingernails—staying my hand.

In the intervening hours, what changes?
The past slaps darkly
                              against the coast
of the immediate, and surety of what
we *would* or *wouldn't* do becomes a matter
of taste, not of truth. Learning to love is not the same
as being fed.
                    Fingers cleaning, fingers moving
food to mouth: both glisten. A small motion
of the wrist and the minnow slipped
down into the wet pile of squid innards, shining
there like my thoughts
                              on the subject, still
and open-mouthed. She plucked out the ink sac,
set it aside. Pulled the next squid from the pile
and continued her work, slicing, plucking,
setting aside. That evening,
                              I ladled adobo
onto my plate: squid, ink, vinegar, peppercorns.
What we understand of death may be only
that it is a kind of labor, a further, but obscured,
process.

In which the photograph has very little to do with the memory associated with it

—bodies outside
of time—

the bowerbird collects its treasures out of a singular
concern
for their color; in this they have value to him
& he makes of them
a palace of discarded goods

on the glossy page, the blue of the sky reflects
the several halos
of overhead light, multiple suns encircling
multiple related children
bundled up against the bright cold—

I clip together magenta & October,
the quick *wwzzzz*
of a wiffleball bat & the corduroy
of the jacket
I may or may not have been wearing

do not mistake the bower
for a nest—
it is not for nesting

I am not nesting here in Appalachia,
I am building ornament
in the form
of a clattering plastic ball coming to rest at the foot

of a workshop door
dancing in front of that door
saying *here here here here*
I open the door & the wiffleball rolls in, a small hard noise

the shop is our grandfather's
it is a machine shop
it is full to the brim with handmade guns

some of us will go on to see this as an unalienable right
some of us
will go on to grapple ineptly with an admixture
of horror & fascination
& despite this
take anyway the cloud-grey barrel of the rifle

& prop it upon the bower-palace hung round
with photos
of smiling children who may or
may not have been improvising, on that clapboard-
edged lawn, a rough diamond—

bird, you seek to impress
one with whom
you would make more birds—

I seek to unwind my love from its implicit violence
to tilt the photo
such that the glare of the light
obscures none of our faces

In the Morning, in the Evening

My mother's father may have lost his mind.
Each bluing morning the same fish
are in the pond. He says, *I will count
them. One, two. Fourteen. Forty?* and then he forgets,
beginning again. In these recesses, something
battered moves, then is stilled in a stroke.

That's what it is; we know this. A stroke.
A literal wearing of holes in the mind.
Ivy of time, branching greenly across ... something,
and then the searching, watery fishing
for something as wetly marine as forgetting,
dividing loaves, dividing, then losing count.

At first he lost my mother's name, lost count
of his only three grandchildren, every last stroke
of English he had (precious little). Since, he's forgotten
our own memories – time and again he reminds
us of where he went to school, of how he used to fish
with each of us, of how he taught us something

like calculus, its dense theories. Things
like this make us think he could still count
to one hundred in binary, that the incident with the fish
in the pond is why they call it a stroke:
like luck, but only the chance. I'm reminded
thus to take pictures, to write; anything to ease forgetting

if it happens. But let us not forget
the nearly infinite mercy of the table. Something
glistens there in salty permanence, as if our minds
had safer havens, darkened, for which we cannot account.
At dinner, the motions go on like the stroke
touched nothing. Every bone and flake of fish

become familiar knowledge, the fish
itself becoming everything he'd never forgotten.
Look, I am painting with broad strokes
the definition of stillness, of not searching for anything.
In the summer, each soft comma of mango counts
his thumbprint, what's still sweetly ripe in the mind.

And now the cooling, now strokes of evening light something
like a basket of new sardines. Delicate fish. In the counting
and in the forgetting, in the coming of morning, we pay our mind.

Burial at Sea

(for Ray Andrews)

Fitting   the weight of bone-ash
and its petulance   refusal to scatter
forcing us   and our rattled hearts
to make sad-awkward   jokes about
a last embrace   carbon with a will

about static cling   as our pant legs
and shoes go patchy   grey
At Great Pond   my father pours
his father into a lake   puts him out
the smoke from the cabin chimney
becomes   what it is

The difference between dragonflies
and devil's darning needles   or whatever
they're called   is that one has a body
the size   of your thumb
and the other   is so small
and jewel-toned   that we tolerate it

Over the course of many years
I continue to be   terrified
of things landing on me   as I float
in the lake   This is normal I think
it is normal to not want your body
to be docked upon   unexpectedly

Non-human animals   however
do not have   the same hang-ups so
I wonder   what it was like for the bass
to gape suddenly   over duller flies
to come up   through a surface dusted
with a strange pollen   a summer snow

I do not have   the mind of a fish
my nutrients   come from mastication
To my grandfather in the lake
who feeds   the soil that cradles it
I am sorry I flinch   from the scales
flashing greenly   in the rich water

The Result of an Overabundance of Scenery

Rain slaps the metal ceiling of this city as if it wanted inside, as if it weren't already inside. Over the last few sweetish bites of *puto,* my cousin tells me that for my next visit to the Philippines, he'll have destinations lined up, individual pearls linked on pale thread. I chew and think about more time in Baguio, the only place where it occasionally snows. I am tired of trying to avoid phrasing things in terms of precipitation—the soothing cool, its quick and fervent lashings, how it wakes me up at night, exhaling into my ear. A single shell, some *Epitonium.* The dogs in the streets ignore me. The flesh of a coconut, or, unbroken, its muffled sloshing. I fear I will develop a hunchback from stooping.

*

I was buying oranges in the market, shuffling through my *pesos,* when my friend remarked that she had been wondering why all the vendors were speaking English to her, "and then I'm like *wait,*" she said, and pointed at me. I asked the vendor the price in Tagalog, which is really all I can do, and pulled my hood up over my hair. You see. There is weather in every story. The wet breeze of it slides in through the window and smells of salt and charcoal. The wind's let up. Roaming around the apartment, my feet are long and narrow, like my father's. I love my father. I love my mother. So what? Looking for a clean teacup. Dabbing at a spot under the burner. Outside, a huge potted plant has fallen over.

H.O. Andrews & Sons

In the name, the mental being of man communicates itself to God.
—Walter Benjamin

Near the basement door, the enclave
of the linen closet holds the shadow of the feed sack
like the sides of a light box.

ANDREWS
X-TRA PROFIT
FEEDS
manufactured by
H.O. ANDREWS & SONS INC.
Mapleton Depot, PA.

McVeytown, PA.   Mattawana, PA.

After antiquing, my grandmother sits at the kitchen table
and gestures at it, says *I paid seventeen dollars for that stupid sack,*
your grandfather would have killed me

and I am squinting at the sack as one might
squint at a series of fingerprints, each stray fleck
of burlap holding still for its picture.

Forgetting, or its idea, is something like death
in miniature. Standing in my mental being, I do not recognize

my name. I name the sack *coincidence* and the sack
names me *fool*. Each day I pull apart the limbs of my As,
each night, flustered, I perform botched reconstructions, holding

handfuls of dry corn against my ringing ears—

Andrews is our Andrews Andrews is your Andrews Andrews and sons and sons
   and sons—

I am full of mice and I name them *family*.

Notes on the Spine, Pt. 1

At some point

during the period

when my body

was putting itself

together at

breakneck speed

something went

kind of wrong

like not massively

wrong

but enough so

that now I have

to deal with the fact

that physical out-

of-sorts-ness

bends half of me

downwards at all times

as if my back

    were trying to sidle

     away from

          these pronouncements
          I make
          about the cosmic
          conflation of
          body and race

     but nothing

    is sovereign

   and while

scoliosis probably

won't kill me

I traffic in

misprisions

this language

of fracture

and this is why

my T9-L5 want

out

Notes on the Spine, Pt. 2

We hinge like puppets until we don't.
I call my mother to tell her about a new
pain in my knee and she tells me I'm
just getting old,
                    that's just the way things are now.
She's probably right but I hear my dad
in the background saying Thelma,
don't be a bad mom. I probe my patella
on its bed of tendons,
                    my achy hips in their sockets.
You're not a bad mom, I say. Just
a mean one. We laugh. The joke is
that Asian mothers are blunt like
ball-peen hammers,
                    precise in their denting.
That my frame is now wonky
from the repeated blows. Of course
this metaphor makes no sense. Of course
she loves her daughters
                    better than her mother
loved her, but that's a joke now too:
Bimbi! You got fat. I on the other hand
have always been told that I would learn
to love the legs
                    I thought were too gangly and pale,
that I, in some important sense,
would form a lovely shape. No risk of me
getting called a chink on the soccer field.
My mother does not
                    understand my anxieties.
This is fair in some ways: after all,
I have been given everything this country
asks for. I'm sorry your joints hurt,
my mother says. You grew too fast.

IV.

What is expressed here is a feeling of vertigo characteristic of the nineteenth century's conception of history. It corresponds to a viewpoint according to which the course of the world is an endless series of facts congealed in the form of things.

A Brief History of Fruit

These were the years in which I saw myself an apple blushing from red to yellow
and back again. My father puts a box of clementines on the counter. As an
oncologist, he does not grow things, but causes them to cease to grow.
Recompense is a fancy way of saying that we believe in the finite quality of
deeds. Sometimes I sit with a peach under my nose and allow it to change the
air there, an indentation labeled *peach*. At some point, everyone's family had
to deal with the question of sustenance. It's how they answered the question
that leads to both agriculture and geopolitics. I love the multiple ways in which
one can use the word *cultivation*; there are so many things to be coaxed out of
wherever they're hiding. What does it mean, anyway, to live in a country? I
wouldn't know; I go to the store and shop for the avocados that feel like they
might ripen in a few days because I harbor a deep distrust of immediate
satisfaction. I keep telling myself that naming everything that I've eaten will
convince various juries that I am not guilty. Raspberry, cherry, coconut, santol,
passionfruit (dislike), apricot, lychee, mango, blueberry. So many different
centers. Some that you can bite right through, some that you can drink, and
some that will crack your teeth apart. Writing about seeds means also to write
about permission, which could be pretty revolutionary if you think about it.

The Collapse

(Payatas, Quezon City, Philippines, 2000)

At night during the summer, the mountain of garbage would just light up,
and I would say to my husband: "Look, it's like candles are burning. It's like
we are living in a cemetery."
—Maria Luz Ochondra

Is it all right if I just go ahead and say
that the moral of this story
will have something to do
with the scourge of capitalism? Will you keep reading?
Good   okay   then—

One day, after heavy rains,
the garbage rushed down like

like

one day the garbage
                rushed like
                rushed
                it was in a hurry
one day the
        one   day   the garbage

collapsed, scraping itself clean of every person roaming the piles—

***

You're smart.   You can look up the plot.   I have other things to do.

***

Ravine *(n)*: a place where it is difficult
to build condominiums.

HAIL

All hail level ground
All hail the reuse of refuse to create level ground
All hail the innovations of the Filipino upper-middle class
All hail the need for condominiums
All hail Manila's 10,000 tonnes of trash per day
All hail urban migration
All hail the grey economy
All hail hotel chains like The Peninsula and Mandarin Oriental
All hail Pope John Paul II
All hail hamburgers / "a living metaphor" / the EcoPark

"perilous and illuminated city"

"a torrent made of citizens"

Methane *(n)*: rotten eggs; a flammable gas; opportunity
for waste recapture (obsolete).

In a flattering article in *The Guardian*, it is reported that
conditions are improving since the burial
of 300-800-1400-???? men, women, and children
under the unrelenting liquid that death becomes—
The hotel chains are allowing
the orderly picking-through of their trash

A dog
      dead a year
            your last garment

***

One might argue that the market in the form of trash
has presented economic opportunity for those people
who would otherwise be living in rural, as opposed to

urban, deprivation; that the expropriation of farmlands
by the growing need for disposal sites outside of the
capital city is a foregone conclusion and thus it is, in
fact, a chance for those who have no other real means
of doing so to make a living within the constraints (
however unfortunately) imposed upon them by the
realities of population expansion. In this sense, the
mother carefully assessing the rungs of a ladder as
she climbs down from her shack raised above the rot,
her child clinging to her back like a question no one
has yet been able to answer, has been well integrated
into the system of waste management developed and
supervised by a private operator (name declined).

***

Theorize disposability : plastic :: the global South : _____
(I have failed this exam many times)
(For $195 per try, however, you can take it as many times as you'd like)

***

The stillness after disaster sounds the same
as the stillness of peace   i.e.
even silence   has its own silences
each of which in its nest   requires interpretation

A regional delicacy is beaten chicken   the bruising
toughens the meat   rendering the texture more pleasing
to a palate   that prefers to work things over
There is always something   to be furious about
By which I mean   there is always   some way
to outsource   the concretization   of savagery

***

Speakeasy culture has taken hold in Manila, namely
in Makati, which is the only place in the city that can support
the back of a place called "Joe's Meat Shack" opening
up onto tin ceilings, Edison bulbs, and
clear tumblers full of imported gin and sage syrup.
My cousin took me to one, once, beaming—
It's just like the bars in Brooklyn naman!

***

"Property"

We regret to inform you
that all the IKEA furniture you own
will at some point in the indeterminate but middle-term future
rise up against you by way of labeling each of your body parts
with a letter or a number, dismembering you, and storing you
in a flatpack box for easy transport and eventual reassembly.

Please call the store for assistance

Please call your oranges, long showers, and flowers for when
you're very sorry

Please call every abomination by its proper name,
the-distance-between-us-and-ourselves,

present it with a bouquet
hold out to it wan proof

already decaying   already arrested

that the world pushes up
despite itself   that it riots
in color   repeats

The Anglo-Saxons Move to Warmer Climes

I am not afraid, and am always ready to do my duty,
but I would like someone to tell me what we are fighting for.
—Arthur Vickers, Sgt., 1st Nebraska Regiment,
Philippine-American War (1899)

Us neither-nors   have always known:

Some stories don't need   a serial epic.

You want what you want   for wanting's sake.

The Dawn, Suffused with Roosters

(Bato, Leyte)

BEGIN!	BEGIN!	BEGIN!
MORNING!	MORNING!	MORNING!
o mother	my only tether	the dawn is dark
the dawn is	weather	fitful rousing
rising feathers	my skin as scroll	pale as heather
your country	(is it?)	(possession's fetters)
now sunset	blood red	brown as leather

Your Princess Is in Another Castle

(Centre Hall, Pennsylvania)
(four blocks from my grandmother's house)

At the Grange Fair I slip into a jumpsuit made of bells.
I jingle through displays of wicker furniture

prize pigs Xeroxed classifieds for motor parts John
Deere catalogues a city of tents handed down from
white family to white family TV hookups Penn State
flags rabbits chickens all these real American collars—

I do a handstand in a cow stall. I jam myself
into the modified exhaust pipe of a racing tractor.
I swim in a lake of icing it clogs my chiming,
muted by sugar I pull apart monkey bread

all the way home. The grammar of *saccharine*—
science and affect, a way to say that you are
chemically susceptible to pleasure knowing better.

I, court jester. Kicker of straw and credulous
collector of thick pale yarns. In this universe
(we each have our own how many stars
does yours have is yours also ripping itself

apart increasingly) I say *yes* to King Patrilineal.
Throw Your Club Here For A Chance To Win
The Enormous Stuffed Gorilla or Table Of Farmers
Warning You About Yourself. The lowing and lowing—

the sound of double the diamonds and half the crown,
the moo of recognition, the groan of my sick stomach.

Some Mirages of the Heat-Addled

{the beginning of Manila on a map is an ache in the shoulder of the Pacific}

{i've always wanted to shine but perhaps not this much, i am a wrong beacon}

{the air fills its bowls, runneth over, runneth away with its attendant utensils}

{slogging through the day i am the servant of my own legs, their carrying capacity}

{and the sky's density and the sun and the watchtower of mixed parentage}

{itemized, i stand as in front of a mirror for too long, khaki body like a puncture}

{literal swimming in a salty t-shirt, shames of cloth oh hello you're very close}

{dripping is commerce inasmuch as one exchanges drinks with the street}

{coconuts serve as greenish metaphors, hanging as they do usually well out of reach}

{i am not an ad for whitening cream, please remove me from the billboards on the ring roads}

{in the wet shimmer of traffic i hear dimly no, you will proselytize for as long as we wish}

No one needs another poem about the Second World War

It is a
commonplace
that history is received—
nevertheless, the flecks left
behind by the eraser are more
often than not the color of sunburn.
There are two general stances on memory—
fixing cereal for breakfast every morning and
the nationalization of the cereal industry. I do not
understand why these positions are often regarded as
incompatible with one another. I am walking up the
ironwood stairs of my lola's ancestral home, my
hand on the bannister soft with polish. In its middle,
a long, dark wedge creases the wood, a divot that looks
like the drape of fabric, smooth edges and pooling
shadow. Time, in other words, makes surfaces
less jagged, everything else more so. I've heard
enough stories about the embedded shrapnel
to know that in the film version of my life,
there will be salt and metal in every flashback.
Leyte is famous for witnessing the triumphant
return of the American army, General
MacArthur as the Terminator, etc., etc.
When the Japanese soldiers showed
up at my great-aunt's door, my lola
coughed violently, pretended she
had TB. There were U.S. medics
hiding upstairs. Who, in other
words, is saving whom. The
monument to American
heroism in Palo consists
of the General and several

soldiers emerging from
the water like mermen.
We now know the sea
will reclaim them,
as it reaches with
growing swiftness
towards my hand
on this railing
in this house
where I am
drowning
already

Jesus in a Prom Gown

(at the Minor Basilica of St. Lorenzo Ruiz, Binondo, Manila)

He died for our sins, but the revolution
betrayed him. None of the right feet
are washed anymore, none of the bankers'
tables overturned. But the sun continues
to explode above our heads, and the glitter that

issues forth is sometimes real glitter. So: here is
Jesus, standing pin-straight in the antechamber
with a cross slung over his shoulder as if it weighed
no more than a staff of sugarcane. Outside,
the world's first Chinatown rings itself in scarlet

and so does Jesus, swathed in yards and yards
of dime-store fabric, red as luck and heavy
with sequins. He's a pretty date, a white ruff
encircling his neck, his sleeves belling out
like trumpet fanfare. His hands and feet are bare.

Surprise is useful for confessions: I did not know
the proper ratio of wine to water; I realized later
my tendency to see only misery. Forgive me. This
place plinks itself along like a lilting, Catholic
telegraph, relaying light suffering in red rayon—

dot dot dot   dash dash   dot dot dot—
help us, our idols are very much alive but
our enemies are also in power. Jesus faces
the door and shimmers slightly in the heat.
His toes, perched at about eye-level on a block

of granite, have been worn to gold from prayer.
A heresy: this is how you ought to be, the confident
head of a vermillion drag parade. Recalibrate
our expectations for how joyous it would be to give
everyone, everywhere, loaves and loaves of bread.

In which voluntourism

(Bulacan Province)

"Learning by doing"

The story where you begin by saying "actually in our defense"

The story where you are not handing shoes to the shoeless

The story where you and eight of your Fil-Am friends are taken by trikes up to the hills north of Manila and you lose track of where you are until you are in an impoverished rural community and even then obviously you are lost

The story where you know you are not helping

The story where your not helping is in fact the whole point although you will not be told this

"Post-humanism"

There is a communal *carabao*, and you take turns trying to steer her and the plow she pulls through the soil. It is the animal you speak of, because you are more at ease projecting sympathies onto something that doesn't know about it.

"Global warming"

The *carabao* has a calf and the calf knocks over a small banana tree in its romping

The *carabao* has a calf and you can only think of the way in which your t-shirt is a poncho of sweat

The *carabao* has a calf and you fling weeds this way and that

The *carabao* has a calf and will the weeds simply root again where you have flung them is a question you have but you do not know the answer and you are just doing what your eight friends are doing

The *carabao* has a calf and see above and see nit-picking as both a reassertion of a type of hierarchy as well as something you are loathe to describe your host doing to her patient daughters

The *carabao* has a calf and later you reread Bishop's "2,000 Illustrations and a Complete Concordance" and you put your head into your hands

"Here"

Pandan is a grass. The weather is clear. The grass smells like coconut. You can put the grass into your rice cooker and the rice will end up smelling and tasting a bit like coconut. You can also work it into gelatin and milk products; these are a common component of *halo halo*, the national dessert of the Philippines according to most people. You can make *halo halo* when ice is available. *Pandan* is a tall grass. Bushels of it can be tied together with strips ripped from an old shirt. *Pandan* can be given to you by a woman whose field you have incompetently tilled for an hour. You can take this *pandan* from her and you can put it in your rice cooker back in Manila. This backwards gift economy smells a bit like coconut. *Pandan* is abundant. Your concern for her livelihood is also abundant. You eat the *pandan*. You eat your concern.

President Trump, thank you for calling, and good evening, it is night over here

Is it too late?
No it's okay we

        don't sleep much   You are not
a person   at all

          I am
the drug problem. Many countries have the problem, we
     are

        the scourge of
      the Filipino nation

               is the Philippines

    nervous about

rockets and warheads
there's no telling

       Rodrigo? Are we   stable or
not stable?

     not stable, Mr. President

                  a
dangerous toy   for
all mankind

    the

               power

has to be

with   bombs   from the looks of it

We have a lot of firepower   We

could

be crazy

Every generation has a mad man—in our generation it's   you

we can

not

remain   peaceful   a nuclear blast
is   good for
a very good relationship
with   Florida

actually we are
afraid

On another subject   I guess

Rodrigo

If you want to come to the Oval Office, I will love   you

come see

me
Seriously   come over

the

people of the Philippines

will   remain
secret
come see me

Rodrigo

Pastoral

Multiplicities of work, in those green days—

By *field*, I mean both the expanse across which

☐ ☐ ☐ ☐ ☐ ☐ ☐

and the sum of all possible relations between a person
and the objects in their environment

By *environment*,
I mean both this achy wrist and a series of cellars

Father, this is not how I had intended to reference
        the fact

That you are too gentle to shoot clay pigeons

That my eye behind the gun trains itself on testaments
written in a language I barely understand—

Arias of antlers, ammonia bottles, ash from the kiln
that forges the bayonets we stand behind,

      murderous alphabet

By *America*, I mean the sighing sense of moving from body to

☐ ☐ ☐ ☐ ☐ ☐ ☐

as well as a knife worn
        from hunting from sharpening from hunting again

down to the nub

V.

*I have always kept ducks, he said, even as a child,
and the colours of their plumage, in particular the dark green
and snow white, seemed to me the only possible answer
to the questions that are on my mind.*

Next of Kin

The trees have nothing to do with it   the ones
standing sentinel in the midst of cornfields
The ones   we leave   to remind us
that at one time we could have been sheltered

I live in a time of competing utopias
There is one   wherein the seas stay put   and one
wherein everyone looks like me   I read
The New York Times every day is how I know this

It tells me "a small but growing body of research
suggests   that multiracial people are more
open-minded   and creative"   Well
consider me a shopping bag repurposed as a hat

I am nowhere near beautiful enough
to be a root system   the skin on my heels
sloughs off regularly   I walk through the world
staring straight at my deteriorating knees

In other words I am decidedly   not the answer
to a landscape   that we continually destroy
in order to feed a relatively small number
of people   I am not ice cream   nor celery

People don't think enough about rhizomes
like lawn grass   aspen   fungi sort of
Which I suppose   makes sense
as "the common root" thing is a little on the nose

But how lovely these yellow leaves are
I can't help it   I weep at the sight of them
I want so badly to agree with your study
To remake the world   as an embrace in a field

The Garden

(Northville, Michigan)

Springsummer, and the world has left us
with red raspberries and asparagus.

In the cranial space occupied by
my mother's childhood garden, I

think more grew at one point—lettuces,
dollops of eggplant beading like guesses

on the question of soil. It's grown strange,
the mind a near monocrop, a turned page

against all odds. Asparagus like children
if left to stretch past tenderness—then

a feathered riot, high as your waist,
deep as a ruffled pool. We face

into the breeze in the spring
because the world insists on shifting

sideways, the tumblers in the season's lock
clicking like a greenish clock

against the earth's plated casing.
The sustaining keys are ripening

currently both in my head and along
the house, where their late June song

is a changeable aria, the white notes
fluttering beneath. A certain labor floats

in these folds, these lanky stalks,
and then my mother's favorite fruit. I walk

though years of raspberries, red dots
like bundles of tiny, vanished thoughts.

Something come then gone. We grow—
until all that is left is *o, o, o* —

In the Evening, in the Morning

My lola has convinced herself that she has contracted
Alzheimer's, and on the eve of her flight back
to Manila, announced that she would never
be coming back to the United States. The story
of any family life has hooks on which to hang itself,
and this is the unhappy, Filipino unfolding of the end

of one generation. Perhaps she thought that, in the end,
forgetting purifies, releases the sick and contracting
body into innocence, as if the active, conscious self
unremittingly sins, is not at fault, cannot take it back.
This is the scrubbed, forgiven version of the story.
Reality, of course, has another dictum, would never

presuppose such faithful charms, would never
let her be so. Here: she's been predicting the end
of her life for years, reciting time and again the story
about how she has some sort of generational contract
to die at eighty-four, how she was supposed to go back
to God five years ago. What snaps, then, at life itself,

its sorrowful tenacity? Existence contradicts itself:
at once a vise and the thing with feathers. Never
middling when mulled over. Anyways, Lola's back
in Bato now, and has abandoned every odd and end
(including her stroke-damaged husband, whose contracted
mind cannot process, though it tries infinitely, the story

of her leaving) to her children. Two and a half stories
of house. The contents of a refrigerator. The fridge itself.
Endless financial woes, including a signed contract
for a retirement place she bought with no intention of ever
living in it. Upon realizing the diminishing ends
of Lolo's awareness, she emptied his savings, went back

to her birthplace and claimed insanity, her backup
plan for being a poor criminal. Oh my lola, your stories,
your sins. Your savior Jesus, shining there at the end
of all your nights, suffers on the end of your rosary, itself
a calculus of forgetting. Filipino elders are never
wrong; this delights you. But if death is a contract

with truth, then it is also an end that you cannot take back:
tropical contracting, the touch-me-nots shuttering their stories.
Shielding themselves. This chorus, this *never, never, never.*

Your Inbox. Love, Manila

(for H)

FROM:
TO:
SUBJ: The fan herds the noon air like warm, disheveled cattle

around the kitchen to which I am relegated: in a country
where I am no help, it seems my sheets are changed twice daily

FROM:
TO:
SUBJ: After every new book of poems I read

I get a nearly insatiable urge to take a nap, as if falling asleep
on other peoples' work will make me more capable of sequestering this orchard

FROM:
TO:
SUBJ: Outside

a pregnant cat
has been trying
to get into our garbage
for days

FROM:
TO:
SUBJ: Lately, I've been flipping on the hot water when I shower

even though every tall glass here becomes a monument
to sweat –
        I would say that this is fortunate, but I don't
want to lose my tolerance for cold, either, enamored as I am
of sunlight frail and thin, pale as my skin

in that same season
        I miss milk, which is either weird or utterly logical

FROM:
TO:
SUBJ: I learned to say

I've missed you
but the phrase seems too long,
crowded syllables
like sad, slanted doorways

FROM:
TO:
SUBJ: The streets in the evening

I chewed pork on a stick

FROM:
TO:
SUBJ: I think more

and more that if you were here, you might see
tiny bits of me, like crumbs
of rice scattered over the table at lunch
        I might be the laces trailing after an old shoe,
or those useless five-*centavo* coins
squinting up from the street beneath you

FROM:
TO:
SUBJ: What if

every day were sandy
        The minutia of salt's grit on our skin

Elegy for One Who Died in the Decade It Took to Write This Poem About Dying

(for Virgilio Quiogue)

And so there is both process and reflection, the movement
of a flight path and its destination. The ocean's a big
place that carries every conversation along its craggy
bottom. That's what the internet is, anyways, countless
intentions drowned and coughed back to life on this
or that grayish shore. You would have appreciated the
sheer volume of the math required to make all of us
miserable all the time but not that outcome.

As it stands, I'm incapable of thinking about anything
not in terms of language and you were increasingly
incapable of language and I spent my time writing
about that in a state of increasing futility. Here is a list
of the things that you could name: War U.P.-Diliman
Fulbright Princeton Germany Unisys. I have arranged
these things in chronological order because The Filipino-
American Dream is nothing if not relentlessly diachronic.

Deterioration begets repetition begets monologic loss of
certain learned abilities and a reversion to ingrained,
un-rub-outable capacities. In an assimilationist
immigrant family this then begets certain cruel
ironies, such as your loss of English when you had
not taught either of your children any Tagalog. Lucky
for them, aural osmosis is pretty much unavoidable
even in the absence of dedicated instruction.

(To *lose* is to *not recall*, to be unable to shout into
your cupboard full of teacups and have the correct
one reply *that is my name and I am full of variables*)

Now there comes the time of our narration knowing the
        outcome. The time of our tenderness, the length
        of time it took me to figure out that *your lolo is an*
        engineer did not mean *your lolo drives trains.* Which is
        one way of saying that each small *see?* of my mother's
        slippers across the floor in an early room moves
        that small lever under the solar plexus labeled Awful
        Means To Be Full Of Awe. Your nurses called you
        Virgil which is true for all of us. You loved Detroit
        winters and VW Beetles and mashed potatoes that
        Lola made badly and all of this is true for all of us.
        Numbers are also true for all of us but so is the ideology
        of difference. Grief scaffolds like a proof: begin assuming
        not-x, conclude that in fact x, *there*, must be the case.

I. Contemplating a career in ornithology, age 12

The beautiful science: naming, trees of one thing,
then another, then yet another, slightly different—

Spinus tristis   *Passer montanus*   *Suburbus americanus*

There are bird-people and there are not-bird people
and often the distinction rests on whether the idea of

flight makes you feel like yourself or your own shadow

II. The relevant literature

Bird books for beginners are sometimes arranged
by color   the largest section inevitably of brown

the thinnest of green (with even names that sound
rare   *Archilochus colubris*   *Tachycineta thalassina*)

the section on white   omits the broiler chicken
a human invention   now numbering in the billions

In order to locate a bird in a book so arranged
you have to use your judgement as to what color

most of the bird appears to be at e.g. your feeder

you have to say e.g. "that one's mostly yellow"

III. Opening

"A long, descending call, a decrescendo"
"A singular *chip*"

"The distinctive *coo* of the mourning dove is
unmistakable, as is the whistling of its wings as
it takes flight"

To what extent is all of this just general birdsong—

my amateur ears can't hear northeast Appalachia
anywhere   the U.S. must have different

singing trees than other places' singing trees surely

With my book at the bay window   I learn
that I do not appear   in the blue
section or the red section   in the book of sparrows

and finches that are definitely endemic to this region

Fugue in A and D

boots
x
yarn
x

apology
boots
farmland
yarn

dust
apology
dry
farmland

butter
dust
bone
dry

x
butter
x
bone

On Cold, On Green

Mid-November, the mind's steel pail. It tips—

(and what spills from this bucket I've drawn?
a flock of ducks   pale curtains   a berry)

—galvanizes everything. All
that is not gray shifts in sleep at the bottom of its well.

The stray cats, collectively the color of weather coming,
inch closer to the house during these solid evenings

and I sympathize: as the light emaciates, as the puddles
contract, I find myself

in amongst the travel photographs. Here Bohol,
here Bulacan, here a banana tree, somewhere, stretching.

The sun an ocean, responsible for everything.

*Perhaps this is why I have turned my gaze so insistently to blue:
it does not purport to be me, or anyone else for that matter.*

The air so saturated that it falls like cold, pulling branches,
birds' tails, and fabrics' unresisting drapery downwards.

As if anything were capable of being stilled
with the words that name them.

Pyramids of fruit shout under laminate, bob
in their skins on the surface tension. The dust

is specific, a particular wet brown, carrying some smell
suspended so naturally in the aforementioned air.

I no longer know   what I am saying.
It is still and dry. Something creaks.

The sky the color of the sky in winter.

Pagmamano

The word mano *is Spanish for hand while the word* po *is often used in Filipino culture and language at the end of each sentence as a sign of respect when addressing someone older. Put together,* mano po *literally translates to* your hand please *as the greeting initiates the gesture of touching the back of the hand of an elder lightly on one's forehead. An identical tradition is followed in neighboring Indonesia and Malaysia called* salim *and* salam *respectively, suggesting that the* mano po *tradition dates to precolonial times.*
—*Wikipedia*

[citation needed]

there is no word for "sorry" in Tagalog
instead you ask the one you've wronged to let it go

my lola calls from Michigan in the years before repatriating herself—
a proud brownish nut, I've just returned from her Visayan hometown—

we exchange hellos
then suddenly   from her end   *Kumusta?*

the pressure centers in the body

by which I do not mean alternative-medicine-energy-whatevers
but rather the actual places where the nerves register force

can go haywire when a foreign substance like anesthesia or
replacement protein fluid
is injected nearby—

it turns out we are all in some way resistant to healing

my mouth a series of alarms calling to have their batteries changed silence over a cell phone is just normal silence

I say *mabuti!*   I say something in a tongue I've had stuck
to my chest for months   it drew my chin downwards
in many social situations   interrogatives caught in my teeth

I am American in that I unabashedly think
that we make too much of our own long existences
I bow my head to no one   because I often want to die

look I am A+   look I have the keys to yet another house
my lola says *mabuti* po   *mabuti* po

surprised silence over a cell phone is just surprised silence

In which I learn that I will not be moving back to Pennsylvania

Hope is the thing you identify with between the road & the forest

Once I had an X-ray that revealed that my ribs are made of clapboard

In the early blue, each mammal steps carefully into its waiting shadow

Corkscrew willows are popular landscaping trees as we've made them

In our own image, that is, our limbs wound helplessly around ourselves

The girl at the bay window   the corkscrew willow in its bed

Rigorous non-nationalism according to Butler is a prerequisite

For the radical rethinking of our modes of community & belonging

I'm trying to unknot my hands from this fence but could use some help

Won't you tell me that hexes aren't paintings but ancient curses

Won't you tell the girl about the tendrils growing *C*s around her feet

In which there are several half-Asian folks at a faculty meeting

about increasing diversity   and someone says   well as you can see
we are all white here

perhaps we will never figure out the mechanism behind the yawn's contagion
perhaps the truth is

that we are sometimes reminded   that we have not actually been breathing
that our chests are screaming for air

which moves over the vocal chords with the pressure of a train on its tracks
well   but   I'm

the spring crocus   early and purple and cream   a joy and a silence
opening to let the air in

what and the answer is *nothing* and the answer is *everything* and the answer is
a series of silhouettes

against the sharp poster board of one's presumptive motions in a room
perhaps the truth is

that the white   crocus or otherwise   blooms first from winter's fist
that it is not spring

that it is still winter   as we can see   as far as we know   we   we
the quiet of yes

now is not the time   you say yes   you allow the discussion to move on
this is good

see   you are hearing me right now

The Discrete Mathematics of a
Mixed-Race Anxiety Sufferer

Dreaming's consequential syntax pushes the sun
into a sky whose sonatas are thus
open to interpretation—

if rafters of sand ballooned before me like worry,
then the sweeping of a porch takes
to the air variable dusts,

if the anticipatory night clutches evolution to its bluish
pockets, then I think through
the weather as an egg

that will hatch, predictably, the pointed beak knowing
for the first time the contrast
between *wet* and *dry*—

if heat is the failure of matter to fly apart, despite
its shaking, despite its applied
and nightly terrors,

then the core of the earth is a collection of loose change—
if I am of multiple *Herkünfte*
then so is

the ghost upon my chest which tells me *you will breathe
the air I tell you to breathe* be it
tropic or temperate

and lo, I was chased into wakefulness by a lungfish
saying *between between between*
and I say *quit it*

I have enough problems what with my intolerance for heat but
they nevertheless stick around,
eyeing my own eyes—

if this dream moves me into a basket full of spare parts
then I hold out to you my nose,
dare you to place it.

What We Have

We have too many bags   to make it   into the house   in one trip
We have a roof   that gets partial sun   and so   is both bare shingle
And covered in snow   although I guess   that's probably true
For most folks   because what is multiplicity   if not merely   the fact
Of our being in the world   that is   if not merely   two forearms
Touching on a bright beach towel   the commonality   of towels
So then the question   becomes one of the distinctions   between modes
Of multiplicity   of one's relationship   to negation   perhaps it is
The homesickness   intractable   as an aspen stand   objectless
As pebbles   we are to be found   at all temperatures   in the updraft
And the downdraft   we have the nowhere-everywhere eyes   we say
We are always on the lookout   and this is true   and a fib simultaneously
We have Craigslist ads   and grammatical concerns   about conjunctions
Some of us are asked   by cashiers   and some of us   lie down
In the field   both flooded and aerated   and what sayeth you unto us
Besides "I thought so"   we are all   good enough Kantians
To recognize   the minor sublime   to know that danger is often intrinsic
To the fact of the body   that God has a body   we have metaphors
That all seem to be   about math   we know that *All*   is German
For the vacuum   of space   we leave blank   most questionnaires
For what is choice   if not   the origin   of misprision
And what is an ocean   if not   the dissolution   behind the copula

Mango Mouth

When soft appears,
and I mistake the purple rot of the hydrangeas on the counter for their
    sweetness—

O yellow ear, o fortitude, o urushiol.

Toxicodendron radicans sounds like a superhero name,
Mangifera indica more like what it is, the manhandled feral,
and something on the skin of my face cannot tell the difference
and the magic works   and its inverse
and I break out into the tiniest hives.

What speaks like the skin of its own geography?
The organ that we leave everywhere,
that hunches and furrows   dries and slicks
makes us human, or less so—

the calculus of touch, the causality of reaction. That burns and prickles,

that renders invisible

In the story where my hands push the fruit
from its peel, where there's no water at the tap and the stickiness
sings like the blown-down reeds of the authentic,
contact dermatitis serves as a book about indulgence,
about the taking and taking until you're a swollen mass
of the sun that is not yours
of the leaf that is not yours
of the sap

that you insist, I, that I insist I can avoid by opening wider around the
    spoon—

I count them on the bones beneath my limbs:

things I love that cannot touch my lips.

Acknowledgments

Grateful acknowledgement is made to the editors of the publications in which these poems first appeared, often in significantly different form: *Anomaly, The Asian American Literary Review, The Cheat River Review, The Cimarron Review, Crab Orchard Review, Gigantic Sequins, Grist, Harpur Palate, iArtistas, The Journal, Linebreak, Nat. Brut, The Normal School, Philadelphia Stories, Poetry Northwest, Rambutan Literary, Re(Verb), RHINO, The Southampton Review, Sugar House Review, Tinderbox Poetry Journal, Underblong, West Branch,* and *Zoland.*

Thanks also to Lettre Sauvage Press for printing "As in Nowhere, No-One" as a broadside, to *BOMB Magazine* for featuring "Your Inbox. Love, Manila" at *Word Choice,* and to the editors of *Bettering American Poetry* vol. 3.

My enormous gratitude to Diane Seuss for choosing this manuscript for the Akron Prize, and to Mary Biddinger and the rest of the team at the University of Akron Press for both believing in my work and graciously and expertly ushering it to the finish line.

Thanks also to the people who have made me a better poet and thinker. To my teachers: Robert Spahn, John Copenhagen, Christine Perrin, Julia Kasdorf, Brian Lennon, James Brasfield, Langdon Hammer, and Paul H. Fry. To my friends and comrades in writing: Rachel Mennies, Daniel Story, Geffrey Davis, Sarah Blake, Brandon Menke, Monica Ong, Lisa Factora-Borchers, Theresa Jaranilla, and Conchitina Cruz. And thanks, too, to Washington College for its support in the finishing and publication of this book.

For their art and photography, I'd like to thank Debbie Carlos and Rachel Engel.

But most of all, I am here indebted to my family, whose endless love and support and ocean-crossing made this possible, and to Alex, for whom words will not suffice.

Notes

Section Breaks: Claudia Rankine, *Don't Let Me Be Lonely* (Minneapolis, MN: Graywolf Press, 2004), 91; Brian Lennon, *City: An Essay* (Athens, GA: University of Georgia Press, 2002), 31; Conchitina Cruz, *Dark Hours* (Quezon City, Philippines: University of the Philippines Press, 2005), 47; Walter Benjamin, *The Arcades Project (Passagenwerk)*, trans. Howard Eiland and Kevin McLaughlin (Cambridge, MA: Harvard University Press, 1999), 14; W.G. Sebald, *The Rings of Saturn,* trans. Michael Hulse (New York: New Directions, 1998), 248.

"Ode to the Letter Q": see Sharon Olds's "Q," a very good poem from which, nevertheless, this poem does not take any inspiration. http://www.newyorker.com/magazine/2009/08/10/q.

"In a different sky, on a different night": Jennifer S. Cheng, "Chang 'E," in *Moon* (Grafton, Vermont: Tarpaulin Sky Press, 2018), 38.

"Did you hear about that video camera…": The video in question (title: "Camera falls from airplane and lands in pig pen—MUST WATCH END!!") can be found here: https://www.youtube.com/watch?v=QrxPukoJefA.

"The Bath": Joshua Clover, "The Fire Sermon," in *Red Epic* (Oakland, CA: Commune Editions, 2015), 12.

"The Minnow": Li-Young Lee, "The Cleaving," in *The City in Which I Love You* (Rochester, N.Y.: BOA Editions, 1990), 85.

"H.O. Andrews & Sons": see Walter Benjamin, *"Über Sprache überhaupt und über die Sprache des Menschen."* http://gutenberg.spiegel.de/buch/-6521/1.

"The Collapse": The epigraph comes from Seth Mydan's article in the *New York Times* on the Payatas garbage collapse. See http://www.nytimes.com/2000/07/18/world/before-manila-s-garbage-hill-collapsed-living-off-scavenging.html. The *Guardian* article can be found here: https://www.theguardian.com/world/2013/jan/29/manila-philippines-recycling-payatas.

The lines in quotes in the third section are from Anne Boyer's *My Common Heart* (Spooky Girlfriend Press, 2011), http://www.anneboyer.com/wp -content/uploads/2012/02/anneboyermycommonheart.pdf.

"The Anglo-Saxons Move to Warmer Climes": see George Mason University's compilation of quotes from soldiers here: http://historymatters.gmu.edu/d/58/.

"President Trump, thank you for calling..." is an erasure of the transcript of the April 29, 2017, call between Donald Trump and Philippine President Rodrigo Duterte. As of this writing, Duterte's war on people struggling with addiction has resulted in over twenty thousand extrajudicial killings across the country.

"Next of Kin": See https://www.nytimes.com/2017/03/04/opinion/sunday /what-biracial-people-know.html?_r=0.

"On Cold, On Green": the italicized lines are from Maggie Nelson, *Bluets* (Seattle: Wave Books, 2009), 67.

"*Pagmamano*": *kumusta* means "how are you?" in Tagalog. *Mabuti* means "I'm well."

"In which I learn that I will not be moving back to Pennsylvania": see Judith Butler and Gayatri Chakravorty Spivak, *Who Sings the Nation State?: Language, Politics, Belonging* (London: Seagull, 2007).

"Mango Mouth": *Toxidodendron radicans* is the Latin name for poison ivy, which is distantly related to *mangifera indica*, or the mango plant.

Photo: Rachel Engel

Kimberly Quiogue Andrews is a poet and literary critic. She is also the author of *BETWEEN*, winner of the New Women's Voices Prize from Finishing Line Press. She lives in Maryland and is Assistant Professor of English and Creative Writing at Washington College.

Printed in the United States
By Bookmasters